In Gravity's Pull

In Gravity's Pull

Poems by Gail Segal

To dear Barbara —
with love
+ sass,
Gail

IML PUBLICATIONS
NEW YORK

For Leon Schein—
who made it possible to land

Cataloging-in-Publication Data
(Provided by Quality Books, Inc.)

Segal, Gail (Alethea Gail), 1952-
   In gravity's pull : poems / by Gail Segal. -- 1st ed.

   p. cm.
   LCCN: 2002110151
   ISBN 1-888959-34-7

   I. Title.

PS3619.E415I64 2002   811'.6
                                        QBI02-701802

IML Publications
a division of the
Irene Murphy Lewis Corporation
a tax-exempt public charity

Book design by Gillian Drake
Cover photograph by David Miles

SHANK PAINTER PUBLISHING
P. O. Box 720, North Eastham, MA 02651
(508) 255-5084

PRINTED IN USA

Acknowledgments

Grateful acknowledgment is made to the following periodicals where some of these poems, at times in earlier versions, first appeared:

Chelsea: "Hunger Universal," "The Well"

Gulf Coast: "Didn't You Know?"

The Virginia Quarterly Review: "The Spell," "Tightrope Walker"

Watercolors by Fulvio Testa: "The Nature of Blues, #2"

I am grateful to The Vermont Studio Center for offering me wonderful residency fellowships. And also to the following writers and friends for their generous responses to the poems: Aleksandra Crapazano, Eva Davidson, Matthea Harvey, Carol Hinrichsen, Alfredo de Palchi, Carol Peek, Pat Mangan, Alexis Quinlan, Frazier Russell, Martha Rhodes, Fulvio Testa, and Michelle Wyrebek. For her insight and close reading of the manuscript, I am very grateful to Ellen Bryant Voigt.

Bold thanks to dear patrons, I. Murphy Lewis, Janet Lewis, Alethea Segal, and to the late William B. Griffin.

And my deepest gratitude to Paul Chatelus for the possibilities offered by his love and companionship.

Contents

III. Love's Fragments

IV. The Fall

Didn't You Know?

The world is a stone tied to a string,
the extra thread of a violin maker.
Catapulted into the air
through a doorway of time
we are one long toss in gravity's pull.
The twine untangles itself as skywriting
through the well of the universe, humming.
For years, men who watched the blade
in the center of town
chart the sun's course
predicted the world's end. But there's no end,
only the tug a man walking the dog at dusk
thinks belongs to him, and then—
the breakneck speed of revolution
whirling us back in dizzying turns
into the maker's hands.

I.

Even The Moon Rises

Apple Story

Only one of them wanted light—
those early dwellers, corralled by the dark,
satisfied stumbling
from tree stump to gravel bed
leaving the earth's signature
on ape-rounded shoulders and hairy knees.
Already the hulk shadows clung to them
as they fled the soft motherlight,
splitting and doubling over the ravine
where rains collected and stood.
Only one bathed in it, pleased, finally,
by the edge of things: scales of bark
planking the trees, coarse reeds flattened
by the slither of snakes. What pleased her most
was the sheen on the skin of that round fruit,
bobbing and dangling in the moonlight,
not yet but almost a color.

Tightrope Walker

I am not what you think: mindless.
My father read aloud each day
the poems of Pushkin. He read to us
as we traveled, my sister curled like a kitten
under his coat. Even now, if you ask,
she recites, word for word,
her favorite. First Russian, then English,
just like father—same rising of tone—
as if it were poured into her sleep.
These words make forks in each road of the mind.
They reach in all directions
like lanes we traveled to tent sites
on the outskirts of forgotten towns
where animals, agitated in their stalls,
fed on hay and oats. Nothing is simple.
I warm my muscles with hot rags,
stretch in the half-light of morning.
Physically I am strong, agile,
but this is not the essential. I can concentrate.
I can quote Pushkin. I can follow the words
to a meaning, and then further,
where there is no net below.

The Well

for I. M. Lewis

In the dream, I am a well.
A woman looks into me
with long glances.
I give her skin, smooth as papaya,
hair the color of straw and eyes
full of questions. Each ripple
from turbulence underground
shifts her view. There is also wind.
She is old. She is young. The water
changes every conclusion. I am satisfied
so long as I am full. My source
is not known to me
though I replenish with rain
and where I am deep,
store darkness. I have held
over a thousand faces to light,
each one different, each one,
the same thirst.

Lolita's Part

I have this skill. A man wants his tired face
mirrored in my youth,
I find the sore spot, indentation of need,
fill it with praise, adoring glances.
What he refuses to see is my will
in a fixed state of adolescence:
unwieldy, slippery, hiding like a winter reptile
in the culled out mud hole of a lake. I charm.
I elicit favor. What I want: food, fast cars, travel
to places tribal or tropical.
I say I am loved. It is something.
It is a weight strapped to my ankle
against which I test stamina, speed,
endurance. I have the advantage.
I will outlive them. Obstinacy will end.
Life will lose an edge of its meaning. Even then,
I will not say *yes* easily or grow breasts.

Road

All day as she sat by the road,
a stick in her hand,
swaying it like a wand
through the air, nothing changed.
Not currents stifled by
thick columns of heat,
not fat boy in the street,
hugging big dog past all
boundaries of affection,
not even the sad set of birds,
perched on the wire,
black blossoms against sky.

But by the time dusk covered the road
and the screen door clapped
behind her the fact of dinner,
soft crystals of dirt
had swiveled and ridged
under her feet
to match the shape of her shoes.

Sky

in memory of Jim Humphreys

Clouds make their conference
circling the sky.
She will not move until they pass over
only there's no wind, so they sit like sheep
at the edge of the horizon
as she lies in a vacant field under blue.

Darkness comes. Still, no sign.
She knows her mother will wonder
what on earth has been keeping her,
but she has made this promise
in the broad daylight of an open field
and so, to god.

This seems to her without knowing the word:
ominous. She sings herself to sleep
with simple lullabies. When she awakes
to the light just before dawn
the entire sky is gray.

Mud

Behind the long row of weed grass
squatting in dirt
she hides from her relations
who come every Saturday to visit.
She strains to hear the car engine,
notice of their leaving, but today,
bending on toward night, she hears nothing,
just a hum in the gnat swarm,
crickets rehearsing
near the river bed a mile off.
Buggy and wet on this Savannah slope,
she purrs her irritation,
cursing the way blood-folk
claim so much time. Each week
she scampers like a rabbit
to the foot of the hill,
a fugitive, running from prayers they say aloud
in her presence, prayers she's terrified
someone will answer. She
has her own god, who comes
each spring as a river rising,
swamps the grassland, soaks
to new growth the thorny briers.
All summer they snag her clothes,
pluck ripe blood from her wrists and ankles,
knot and thicken until only low animals
crawling from the creek can get through.

Fish

Desire is what she wants, not its object,
not her father in Irish tweeds
draped from hips no wider
than the girth of the hobby horse
she rides to Banbury Cross or any crossroad.

It's Christmas morning.
She wants to be weak, to dissolve,
lose her place, her breath, dry bone of spine
jellying into fish as she kneels
beside her father.

His face is smooth, sweet with Old Spice
scenting the air already heavy
with cinnamon and spruce. He's occupied
with interlocking pieces of a red wooden horse.
He's all intention. His mind is elsewhere.

This is how she's able to come close,
so close her child hands, plump and sweaty
could reach through the light flecked with dust
for his hand or thigh
tightening under her fish palms of desire.

She holds them in her lap,
folded like a prayer that nothing—
not mother in the kitchen or sister

drowsy on the sofa, not the child she is beside him,
will disturb the molecules of this moment.

Flushed, melting, wax without shape,
a jelly fish riding the white water.
Over her, waves are breaking. She doesn't yet know
that she has tentacles. Who will tell her
that tentacles have stinging cells?

BROTHERS

And the Lord said, What have you done?
—Genesis

Long before the tribe divided
and subdivided land,
before Red Seas parted
and stones brought down from the mountain
were sanctioned as law, there were only two brothers
with even portions of plush ground,
even numbers of fish, fowl, even rows of trees—
fruit-bearing sycamores,
seed-bearing pines—everything even
between them, as if each blade of grass,
each square patch of low lying mist,
each strip of horizon
had been counted, measured, sliced
in equal proportion.

You could call it fate,
but one of them looked to this wide reach of land
carpeting the valley and was happy. The other
saw only his brother's face reflecting joy
and it bore into him like infection,
or a tumor moving as a mass through his blood
where it lodged in his heart, soured,
grew stiff, made the pounding muscle
cramped and sore. By then,
he had something real to moan about

while his brother's heart
weighed less than one plume
from the bird he sang with every morning,
less than one lock from the smallest lamb
he took inside his cloak.

Too much singing at sunrise
sent the heavy-hearted brother to the shed. He found
the heaviest tool, leaden and blunt.
In the dry heat of noon, his shadow behind him,
he waited for his brother on the path.
He had to do it. Otherwise,
how could he have known
that what he wanted
was not the land, the sky, the trees blossoming
into fruit. He did not want the lamb
snorting inside his jacket. He did not want
his brother's heart.
He had to do it to know
that what he wanted looked like *hate*,
and he would kill for want of seeing it
in his brother's eyes.

Hunger Universal

You want me to talk about Jakarta?
bony children with gnat-eaten eyes, faces paled
and gray in the breadline of Sarajevo.
I'm here to talk about *myself. My* hunger.

What have you seen to equal it? Crumbs loose
on the papered shelves, refrigerator
humming, empty, not even tired lunch meat
or limp celery, I eat the table, instead, slat by slat,

chairs covered in a bright red,
eat the hook rug, shred by shred,
lamp stand and crunch, light bulb with its filament
and wire. I eat the birdbath in the courtyard, planter

with hydroponic soil, root-stem and fichus,
xylem and phloem, the borborygmus is percussive,
a five piece band on New Year's Eve. I eat
the ballroom and noisemakers, centerpieces of flowers

each petal an aphrodisiac, a communion wafer,
a whipped cream of snowcaps on the mural
in the lobby, mountains below, granite and stone.
I eat hard bones of children from Jakarta,

already underground beside their mothers,
charred skin on faces in the breadline.
I gnaw on knuckles of hands held out to me
twisted by ulnar drift and the drift of gravel

drowning cities like St. Louis, then
I eat St. Louis with its tenderloin of ground buried
underneath. Eat. Eat. With the whole earth inside,
I lick my chops toward stars, galaxies,

clumps of sugared light in the heavens and
god peering from the end of a long hall of universe
says, *My how plump you are.* With one last gulp
I swallow his numinous shadow.

Desert

in memory of Stuart Browne

In the desert she counted stars.
It was the night they left her there,
the night the sight of that gold sliver of moon
rising out of lava rock in the canyon
lured her more than a mile away.

Counting, she named them,
not their given names in Greek,
but *Madscar, Wildwhim, Frozen Note*,
syllables puffed from her lung's fresh heat
into the stone-cold darkness.

For hours, this glossolalia,
sounds so sweet that when she saw
in the deep crease of night, headlights
like diamond eyes of a snake
crawling up the road, she thought of them as stars
and gave them names.

What Truth We Are

in memory of David Miles

What truth we are
is nothing more than bones,
circuitry of blood, electrical matter:

judgements, thoughts, small shocks,
lights that flicker before the fuse goes.
The world is strobed. One second

we know the edges, the next
who can find their way to the door?
Better to close our eyes

and imagine truth.
It looks like a road bent upward
alongside a creek, spilling out

into a pond where the land
gives way. Leaves are making their mark,
flapping and falling. One blue heron

deep in contemplation
occupies the pond. Restless for wind,
she lifts her heavy cape of feathers

then her body, toward the sky.
Everything is rising, rising or falling,
rising and falling: wings of birds,

leaves, shadows of leaves,
breath from two boys in the field
baling the hay, eyelids

governing sleep. Even the moon,
lifted over the blue ridge before nightfall,
rises, as does her lazy concubine,

the tide, lapping on the shoreline
of the truth's outer edge,
far, far away.

II.

Hinges in Time

Fire

Fire reddens our faces
in the big gray house by the river. It's Christmas.
We eat walnuts out of brass bowls.
Grown-ups drink Scotch on ice

that rattles in glasses
they fill and refill into the night. My sister and I
hide in the stairwell—
just one expletive, that's all we need

to double us over in muffled snickers
and snorts. We are snooping through boxes
under a tree that rises to the ceiling
three times our size. Our faces fatten

in globes of red ornaments. Grown-ups
smoke cigarettes; their talk circles and widens.
We eat oranges by the fire,
tossing peeling scraps into flames.

Fire hisses, snaps, heats my back
in a good way. When I move to the sofa
and lean into my mother
I am warm against her. I am still warm in the car

riding dark streets by the river home,
and warm still in my bed
waiting for Christmas to end, and the day after
I am cold for the first time since twigs,

log stumps, branches chopped in the side yard
of that big gray house by the river
were reincarnated, with everyone and no one looking,
as fire.

Night Ride

No one will remember
the night
my father and I
rode down the beach
at low tide. Music blared
from the boardwalk,
girls with bare midriffs
clutched, in one arm,
stuffed tigers,
in the other, boys
who targeted cardboard ducks
for them. Tomato red people
in short shorts
cackled with laughter
in just the way
everything under the broad lights
was harsh. To our right
the world was measureless darkness.
We could hear
the loose skirt of surf
sliding its hem across sand
and just see
faint markings of ripple print
on shore. Farther out,
glints of phosphorous
flickered as borderlight,

as my father and I said nothing,
as we rode between this convergence
in unbendable silence,
stopping just once
for the boy Dad said
had too much boardwalk,
dazed at the edge of the surf,
his car already a foot deep
in a saltwater sludge
sure to eat through,
before dawn,
the muscle of tire.

Second Story

On the second story of an old hotel,
between the Old Fort and Old Jail,
in the oldest city of the New World
I was conceived. They were zany
with love, as they danced to music made
with castanets and maracas, as they drank
the nectar of stars from the Fountain of Youth,
as they climbed circular stone stairs
arm in arm, moon sweating its sweet milk
into the sky, night polishing the sand.

In their second story balcony apartment
nine months and ten days later,
the rhythm of castanets they called my heart
began to flutter in a syncopated beat—
a bird, trapped inside a cage,
hurling itself in repetitious thrusts
against an openwork of ribs and spokes
before collapsing. My skin,
the blue of ocean waters that rocked
the Spanish sailors in their
wooden vessels to shore.

No movie magic in the shrill
distemper of my mother wailing for help,
my sister paddling around the floor

like a puppy looking for pockets,
while the woman next door,
I don't even know her name,
brought me back to life. What
must have settled into their lives,
that summer evening,
when, finished with dying,
I slept like a baby. What misgivings
seeped into the caulking
between kitchen tiles or strained
like islands of light
through slats on the jalousie doors?

No wonder my father took her dancing that night,
and many other nights, took her
from their balcony apartment with its bad breath,
its sticky baby dreaming in the bassinet
of hinges in time, of doors as light as dust,
opening and closing from world to world.

Looking for Love Made Easy

I fell in love
for one tired evening
after a fever picked my bones clean
leaving me nothing but necessary.
He was fine in his fast car,
drinking from the long-necked bottle of rum,
driving like a seizure along the coast,
slowed in Mississippi by night miles of white fog,
liquid and amorphous.

We made it to the Florabama Bar
by 2 am, his friends dancing on their knees
in Alabama, drinking straight shots
across the border—past the last call,
last dance, last mall of men
who'd wake up tomorrow
without one still-framed
sense of this place, this hour, the face of the fat man
in the Iron Rock, Arkansas T-shirt
belting out what was left of the blues.

Our script of booze, bad car, beach road,
beach party ingenue had me gracefully,
like a bay swan lifted off the water,
opening myself for what was loud and strong
like music he filled the car with

two days later. From the ferry look-out,
as we crossed the great Gulf,
dividing back roads of back water,
who was I hoping to find
underneath the kid skin leather of his jacket
that bellowed like a sail,
who was I, road girl, girl of the night,
girl with the pockets full of found pennies,
who *was* I to think I'd find
buried beneath his double-daring,
extravagance of heart?

The Spell

The night after we first met,
after ghosts of air
rustled blinds in the window
and circled the room
where we sat in easy chairs
face to face, I dreamed
we followed the road
to the outskirts of town,
pavement to gravel, then
dust. We were traveling on foot,
heat from the road, heat
from the sky, and the child
tracing our steps with a stick
fainted under the spell of it.

You carried her in your arms
like a bride over a threshold,
setting her down in low grass
when it was time to rest.
All night I dreamed you,
lifting and lowering the child,
her blonde head tethered to a body
by the lace of her neck, veins threaded blue
to match the sky that hovered
above us. All night,
walking with you. What was

44

our destination? Where were we going
when the road broke through
to morning: bed, lamp,
book pressed open on the bedside table,
not you, but emptiness beside me?

Argument

Although,
the same moon rises above us
you are drifting through dark corridors
on slow, deep breaths of sleep
while the lazy glow of day
clings to the city sidewalk
where I stand. Furthermore,
it is already your tomorrow
when that first sliver of light,
that lip of tumescence,
a pouting crescent
with its shadowy face
peers over the clock tower
on Leonard street as moon.
You are dreaming in Verona
as she rises and rises,
moody and sullen,
as the early evening
bells of the tower
chime their seven tolls.
Looking up, looking east
toward an ocean
the moon pushes and pulls
between us, I am inconsolable,
I am wolf and stone,
I am transfixed.

Wake up! Wake up!
The steps of marble
leading from your door
are cold with night, but
above you to the west
she lingers. Here,
she dresses and undresses
in the passing clouds.

Small Craft Advisory

— He showed me old stones
in a Roman wall. He told me stories of painters,
past, leading to him. He uncloseted
at my asking, photographs, his mother
under an Istrian tree in Yugoslavia,
his uncle talking to fish, and himself,
image after image, riding the white water
or standing beside a boat,
made for one traveler.

— When we quarreled, it wasn't exactly a quarrel
but worse: new light in an old room
we'd grown use to seeing in the dark. A bat
flew in the window—black lightening—
darting column to beam, circling one bulb
hung low from the ceiling.

— In the middle of explaining
ourselves to one another
I saw that a sphere dissected
cannot give root or light. Misunderstanding
is not the worst affliction. Of course
Eve plucked the apple, and he bit
its false promise.

— Day takes on a different light
by afternoon. Fog moves to steam rising;
air is sticky with heat. Our bodies lie
face down in the same bed,
arms dangling. The church bell charts time
in quarter hours. When we wake
the air has cooled. We make stiff conversation,
tentative, quiet, small steps
away from a grave.

— Trust me, he says, when just last night,
miles from home,
it came, rain wild with wind,
water slung in sheets, branches
torn from trees thrown to us. The car
rocked and shook, a small craft at sea.
His face said what I knew: danger.

Window of Time

This is my daughter,
my father says, over and over,
to the nurses in blue, a waiting room filled
with men wearing caps, women in scarves.

He shows me the room where they sit or recline,
a banquet room with many chairs, alkylating agents
and antimetabolites, leucovorin, and my favorite, 5-FU,
drip through tubes and needles.

Today they count the cells that managed to survive
the rabid meal healing toxins make of his disease.
We wait for the doctor's "A-OK" and it's here, now,
in this window of time that we face the view.

Down river, morning glazes the sky blue, river,
blue, sleeves of summer grass, lush and green. Palm trees,
like tall flowerettes, line the banks. Bridges break open the light
with girders trapezing as traffic bounds east to west.

Beautiful river city, my father's hometown.
He points to this building, or landing, locating
homes of loved ones, sites of childhood memories,
favorite stories. He has forgotten, for the moment,

where we are, why we're here, until, like a storm
that whips up river suddenly, with thunder
and sticks of lightening, I want to know
what floats on the water just below us.

What are those patches of musilagenous waste,
amoebic clusters of scum,
how did they get there, lapping at every edge?
I see them everywhere water meets the land.

Eternal Life

Once we were singing—my mother,
my sister and me—*like birds in the wilderness*,
sitting on a bench at roadside
next to the Baptist Church.

We were waiting for a bus
that would carry us home
to the weeping willow and mimosa,
lilies scattered like an epidemic,
Spanish moss hanging from the pines.

We were waiting to go home to my father,
who'd be reading in the dark,
to the smell of roast warming in the oven,
potatoes baking, biscuits waiting to rise.

This was a happiness: singing,
singing and waiting, the air
holding its last breath of spring:
We sit at the edge of the bench,
my feet dangle above a ground

they cannot reach. Now, they are swinging.
For a moment, time has no longitude.
For a moment the eternal
has no meaning separate from me.

III.

Love's Fragments

Consent: A Beginning

What did he say to her?
Or was it dumb between them—
gesture, shadow of gesture,
handshapes like swan and snake
in silhouette on the cave wall?
Did he say her name, her name meaning separate?
meaning wide water between them?
Did he pull her dark figure to his body standing
and say, now?
I know she said, slow
if she said anything at all. I know
when she finally reached soft ground,
tufts of grass pressed into her back,
his face full of hunger,
she said, yes. With this
the world was changed.

The Fragments

Open Country

It's open country
when first we come to love.
No houses, no trails
through the thicket of trees,
not even a barn. What animals
are there have not been named.
No way to call them home.
No gate to keep them there.

Ripening

I thought the world would shatter
when my father died. Yet here we are
in the courtyard of a castle
eating peaches in the sun.
The day goes on, juicy and sweet,
we wash our feet in the fountain
and walk miles off the daylight
into dusk.

Current

Your voice is one note: distance.
Far away the wind is fierce.
Here, an afterbreath;
a ribbon rides the current.
I tie it in my hair
as sun steams a surface
that is yellow,
deepens what is red,
the river is nothing but blue,
pushed by a measured hand,
north, north.

Restraint

For the first time today
I write the word *sorrow.*
For hours I held it back
waiting to see
what it might become. Like
a head held under water:
see the arms flailing.

Bride in Venice

We followed her trail of roses
through side streets
looking for the bride. Your friend
filled my straw hat with petals
we tossed into a canal.
You took your hand from mine
to show me the clock tower.
After that: even the little islands of rose
floating in a dirty canal
disappeared.

Exegesis

It's true.
You read me like a book.
But why do you have to say
each word out loud?

Cold Feet

I come back to you.
You are all I have.
My shoes are wet
from rain soaked streets.
I will not take them off.

Sightseeing

What could I show you
that you haven't seen?
Look at the sky.
Each day it changes.

Love's Economy

When the past calls
as a woman you once loved,
I flinch. I know how you cling
to what is behind you. I imagine
filling bowls with fruit,
baskets with bread, guarding the present
with abundance. Rim to rim they line
shelves, tables, countertops,
desks, drawers, chairs, hallways,
doorways, streets, highways, bridges . . .

The Tomb

On the third day
after your leaving
nothing rises. The air
is a stone. My bones
won't move from the bed.
The sun bores a hole
in the day by mid-morning.
When will it rain? When
will the clouds
gather their good will
and cover the sky?

Atomic Cloud

You hold me at bay,
like Pluto kept at cold distance
from the sun.
Have you forgotten?
Pluto is a god.
He makes the widest orbit.
Or think of that cloud
and tell me:
where is its periphery?

Weather

Everyday you peer through the blinds
hoping. Like weather,
I disappoint you.

Undertow

Under this skirt
you crumple in your hand
you'll find an ocean
of insistence.
I warn you.
I warn myself.

Amphibian

You want me to be this way
and/or that. Remember,
I was born in a swamp.
Make up your mind:
land or water.

Infidelity

I see you need them:
the other women.
I need them, too.

Communion

Where are you now?
Living like a monk, you say,
behind the church walls
in Verona. I am here
without simile,
waiting.
Tell the authorities in Rome:
bread is no substitute
for flesh. Wine, even last night's
thick, full-bodied Merlot,
leaves me longing.

Entropy

Gout, arthritis, cataracts
of the heart. High sun
throws harsh shadows.
Colors fade over time.
Do you remember
the way our hearts opened—
a wet field of red poppies
in that early light.

"Without Contraries There Is
No Progression"

Your hands cover your ears,
so much like the siren
swelling the street
is my voice
reminding you of our differences.
I stand next to you.
My blood, refusing to clot,
cleans its empty house.

How We Die

On the way to Asolo
a sky turned orange between us,
stones of the cemetery, pink
and alabaster windows, pink in the chapel,
melted a late day light
into gold. We didn't touch or speak.
Women washed the graves
of two young men,
cut long stems of roses
one by one.

Listen

There are days, today is one,
when every word I say to you
is a divide. Speech or silence?
What's the difference?
Only this: a river moves.
Stones stacked as an arena,
standing for two thousand years,
do not.

Friction

For days,
we jiggle, twist, turn, push,
hoping to find our way
into the same room.
Who can tell us
how to keep love from jamming
the bolt and tumblers of the lock?

Consideration

I see you have forgotten
the first rule of loving me:
Do not poke a poisonous snake
with a stick.

No Landing

Tonight you call,
an ocean again between us.
I wait for words to sail
across its salty surface
into my open heart. What comes
toward me: a freighter
carrying old cargo looking for port.

Melt My Heart

My laughter, you say, is rain
after years of drought,
dust washed from streets,
each cobblestone polished
like a tooth. These words
pry open my heart. Inside,
a river rises as it thaws,
tearing away city walls, pulling
chunks of calcified stone
into its stream.

Peak

It's October. Colors burn
on the farms upstate. Here,
leaves don't even bother.
Brittle from so little rain
they curl in half and yield
to wind. Already, a rustle
under my feet. We want passion,
the bright fires. Look at these trees:
we have to water the ground.

Fight

We do it anywhere now,
in front of anyone. People run
for cover, guard their glassware,
plates. They know that fire
feeds fire. But I remember
the bonfire field
across from the high school stadium.
Each year scorched ground
grew back a deeper green.

Last Chance

We carried it full from the well.
Did we notice the water
sloshing and spilling? Now what?
Who could go again to the source
carrying such thirst?

New Year

After drinking, dancing, smoking
cigars, whitewashing grievances
we're home. Not yet daylight, it's my idea
to spread the Tarot face down
across the bed. You draw the card
for strife, mine: sorrow.
We finish the champagne.
Cheers! Cheers! into one another's arms.

IV.

The Fall

The Fall

When I fell down I thought,
might as well stay here. It was night

and no one saw. I was alone
when wet leaves matted

on grass curved to make a slope
unsteadied me

into a slip and tumble.
Sprawled out, I looked up

into the dark. I saw
black bones of tree

between me and sky
lit end to end with glitter spray

and where Milky Way paved its path
a heavier spray, a second coat.

I wore only sweaters, two,
and it was cold. I knew

I was a fool
to go on lying there—
ground, wet; breath, vapor; bruised
from the fall, no moon,

just tree stripped of plumage and,
at the edges of earth,

sky kneeling.

33 Measures and a Dream

in memory of Bill Griffin

1

Don't think I want this trouble. Calculus of feeling,
x-ing, y-ing to infinity. Afterlife: I know what happens.
You go. The ones you love grow smaller, smaller, heads
bent over numbers, integral, not integral, straining
to measure inside the curve.

2

In extending light I fly west to you. Even so
almost at once, the sky goes dark, a million lead stars
poke through skin stretched tight as a drum over the heavens.
They tell me tumors bloom like phlox across your chest.

3

I see from your study you have no plans to die. An open pen
inks onto paper. Unsulphured apricots fresh from the market,
unpacked. Numbers remain untallied. Above your desk,
shoved to the window—acres of green, fences bobbing
over the hill, a plow readies the ground.

4

Not the rock band from the eighties, raucous, violent,
but a long thin needle jabbed into your back—
this is what they'll do today to stop your dying. Noiseless.
Outside, sheets of pelting rain, a clamor, more on its way
from the coast.

5

Men who love you gather strong, move you onto your side,
lift you to sit, feed you ice. Women wipe your body
with cold rags, rub eucalyptus oil onto your feet.
For three days you are the Christ, limbs swollen, bloated belly,
naked under one tangled sheet.

6

The day I travel home you mutter strangeness, *get serious,
my pants, one way trip.* Alone with you, saying goodbye,
you open wide your eyes looking through me when you say,
Five long days without one good drink.

7

At midnight, flying above Missouri, the Chinese woman next to me
recites her prayers, rotates through her hand a band of beads—
clacking, clacking, clacking. You sit straight up, I'm told, a bolt
from the lassitude of sleep and ask your brother, *Why am I dying?*

8

The weather clears. Contraction. My body holds cold
from that first night, window opened in your study. Here, now,
a stream, jetted white loosens behind the weathered green
of Woolworth's tower. We met one day for lunch beneath its shadow.

9

You're talking more and more your wife tells me, chemicals brighten
like fire in your veins. Remember the yellow dress I wore the night
we watched the wire walker eat those massive flames. You smoked
grass. We sat on a park bench til four am. What did we say
to one another?

10

Paul comes to bring me silver found behind our bed, reading
over my shoulder the nothing on this page. A pasty gray morning
and staring blankly seized me. Now it rains. No word from you
on the west coast to quiet my mind. The soul is in the feet,
I remind you in my dream.

11

Finally, we speak, your voice, low, deep, rising out of ground
you nearly fell into. *We have a lot to talk about*, you say.
I am quiet. And then, unable to resist the future:
You and Paul come to California in August like we planned.

12

The strong arm of a crane rises, diagonal of black, corner to corner
through my window frame. Men in hard hats bare their chests,
tugging the hook, looping hook to the wire, girder rising, rising.
I'm not working, you reminded me, *Call any time.*

13

Gone: the metallic taste, now just a lump of hard candy refusing
to melt. Sack of grain on my chest. I know the earth will open herself,
your bones are not a problem. Grey granite deep in the quarry
was once a mass of molten magma—living, breathing, burning.

14

The morning after we talk they open you end to end. Three holes
steroided into your stomach. What were you thinking
wearing yourself so thin? Now they enter your room with gloves,
masks. White count. *Skin is a nice idea*, Paul mumbles in his sleep.
Even sticky skin, and without sheep, he's under.

15

You all but disappear with children under foot. Paul's kids are here.
The good thing about your dying was the world in focus, peopled
with strangers, constellated as friends over night. We scribbled
our names on scraps of paper. Hurrying back to Paul, I saw that he,
too, for days, took the big dipper in hand.

16

The weather changes, sun builds its layers, like paint,
into grayish-white, low ceiling without borders. The crane revs
its engine all morning. I don't remember what I wore that Saturday
I walked a hundred city blocks to you. We thought my nephew
was dying. Who knew then what death was? A haze.

17

Free to speak, I unpack it all: arms swollen, blue at the needles holes:
atavan, morphine, glucose, plasma, chemicals not yet named,
and cathetered to the worm flopped between your legs, a tube
leading to another see-through bag. The soul is in the feet,
I've tried to tell you more than once, and they were swollen, too.

18

It can't possibly be this hot in California. What do you do all day?
Sun photosynthesizing leaves against that window. Aren't you tired
of light coming through? Every ten minutes a nurse. And the questions.
The old one has no answer. Death is not particular,
though I swear it has an essence, like perfume:
an odor that changes with the person who wears it.

19

Like a coat pulled tighter around the shoulders, sky moves in;
that green blemish of Woolworth, spiking the sky, obscured. I call,
your wife says infection. Workmen walk the beams
like high wire. One torches the joints. The other straddling,
sands the surfaces, leans face down, body wrapped around steel.

20

Heat alert, the radio announces. We walked the river after dusk,
air dead and weighty. Across the water from the west a tower of smoke
spiraled in our direction. Still, children undressed, rolled in the grass,
darted through jets of the park's sprinklers. Paul tore lavender petals
from a stem, rubbed his wrists together—a sticky sweet.

21

Scratches of blue, thin scratches peer through the clouds. You're home.
Nurses watching over you but you're home. Holding your own,
they tell me, white count rising. What's it like—being there?
Slowly, the earth spins you toward the sun. In just three hours
the mist will lift to show you land washed in green and mustard grass
in patches on a hillside drenched in dew.

22

They wheel you room to room inside the house. Outdoors,
around the house, you take in every view—horses grazing
in the pasture near the road, plow upturning soil, roses, lilies, grapes
plump beside the pond, land dropping into an endless valley.
You tell them to remove your shoes, your feet in summer grass.
That feels good, you say, *turn the sprinkler on:* your feet
in wet summer grass.

23

Word came early from many voices. You're dead.
A gurgling rising through your lungs, they said. It must puzzle you
to see us turn devotedly toward your body. Scarce remains.
You're free. We're trapped with cold carnage, memories raveling
like a sweater sleeve. What of that warmth?
Holding your hand through SoHo streets, all the shops were mine.

24

Foul weather, a storm promised that never comes.
Barometric inversion. You must laugh to see us paining ourselves
over changes in wind, or tide, clouds, no clouds. Still for us,
we're here. Straining for a better view of the horizon.
As far as the eye can see.

25

They take their time, workmen, straddling steel beams, plugging pegs
into joints. Do they think they have forever? Your wife's brother says
he saw your ghost, just today, staring at his arms in the shower.
Yes, we still have arms. Your's punctured, swollen, are lighter now,
not even wings, a vapor.

26

Patron, brother, ally friend, do you remember lying in Central Park?
Sitting among the roses in your garden? Or stretched out
at the foot of your bed, twenty years of taking the world's measure
with conversation. *We have a lot to talk about*, you said, last to me.
We never spoke again.

27

Your wife calls, friends one after the next, eager to connect.
My mind crawls deeper into that circle of weeping willows, where,
as a child, I gathered a confederacy—dolls, animals, stuffed and torn,
propped on a mat of pine straw. Drooping, leafy limbs strain sound,
light, even memory. Only mine let through.

28

More sky, air from the north, sunlight baking warmth into walls.
Pounding has begun across the street, pounding, grinding, sizzling
from the torch, searing sheets of metal they lay across the beams.
This is change: not to see the ground underneath. Still,
I can't get it straight what you mean to me. Light keeps
bouncing off each surface.

29

You can't imagine what you miss by not being here—olives,
feta cheese, saussison, almonds from Bazzinis, cupolas lined up
in rows of four, street fairs, sidewalk sales, laundry on a line,
white barn in need of paint, church spire poking through tree
tops after dark. Shelves of grass, bushes, trees in unforgotten rows,

30

or buildings stacked to height against a summer sky, that moon
dangling, forbidden, like dimestore candy. You missed
the opening of Kubrick's film, *Eye's Wide Shut*, he missed it, too.
John John Kennedy missed it by a day. Kieslowski by four years,
Tarkovsky died long ago and yours the only name with a "k." Mistake.

31

What? I'm not listening to you? It's true. So tell me something
to help me with this bumpy ground, every road in need of work.
Sure, you see what's critical, that is to say essential, vital. So tell me
what matters. But I tell you, it's just information. Here, every tribe
has a book—a legion and a book.

32

Workers bang metal sheets into place. Numbers on the clock climb
toward my next appointment. Inside a terrible mix of feeling.
Here we say *sadness*, but don't forget the darker oils—envy, rage,
desire stretched like tar from the tree, to punish what hurts.
Stirring, stirring. Air thickening again with heat, slowly. They say
tomorrow will be worse.

33

Do you feel his presence, your wife asks. Bryan, too,
clear across the world is sure of it. I feel nothing. A nothingness
that once was you I pile memories into, like a child
stuffing her wooden chest with toys, jamming them in, jamming,
so full it won't shut.

   —and a dream

You appear finally in a dream on a street with houses, walking
door-to-door at dusk with another man, like Mormons selling Bibles,
or canvassing, god knows what cause this time. When I see you,
I know you're dead, and wonder if you'd will to me the smoke blue,
long sleeved T-shirt I took from your study that cold night

while you were dying. I don't ask—you are at such distance,
laughing your way up a driveway to the door, wind lifting its arms
through tall standing pines, street lamps opening their tents of light
onto potholes, lesions in the road, and ahead, a dented guardrail
where two deer nibble at overgrowth bordering the sharp turn.

In Gravity's Pull

I sit at the edge of the world, on a rock
at a ledge, below, a river; beside me, a man.

A cross rises from the peak we have climbed
all morning. People with different languages

lumber or sprint behind us to the top. Children
are in view—laughing. A father quiets them as if the air,

clear for miles, commands arrest. The man beside me
does not speak, but rides the slope of memory

to his childhood. I follow the mind of the river
as it bends beyond the curve of mountain stacked

with snow even in summer. Cicadas are racketing the silence
with a ceaseless friction and the tinkling of the bell cow

tells me she has led the Guernseys up the pebbled path
to the barn. The farmer with his son waits to tug the juices

from their tits. I sit restless, idle, on a massive mountain stone
cut by a river. If my shoulders could turn to wings

and fan out over the ravine, I'd ride long ribbons of breeze
down to the muddy flats at the river's edge,

to the town which borders it, where grapes
fatten on the vines, where bread rises

on a narrow kitchen counter, where a man and woman
tumble in love's knot, their sheets a wreckage,

their afternoon, exhausted by refusal
to be anywhere but in the sweat and salt of this world.

The Nature of Blues

She leans into a pool of mercury
hoping to find her face.
What she sees: a slick, unyielding
surface of silver, just more mercury,
opaque refusal. At the water pool,
late day sun burns shelves of lava
from the lake's reflection,
trees, too, have gone silver,
then black. Above the rocks
shouldering in recline
a deepening blue tarp of sky
takes over,
giving nothing but itself,
giving all of itself.

Dusk has its own language
that ends in a shower of stars.
Before this rain
light coaxes each shape to sleep.
Colors speak for themselves.
Yellow shrieks
like a chill ushered to bed
before dark. Red makes vicious,
maniacal strokes
over the last hills, over sky.
Blue is the last word,
favored, dominant, forfeiting gradually
its vast supply.